THE AUTHOR...

Beryl Anderson is a most successful textile designer and creator — but behind the luxury fabrics and outstanding furnishings associated with her name is also a very busy, practical housewife and mother. After studying art as a girl, she took courses in textile design and textile yarns at East Sydney Technical College and afterwards worked in one of Sydney's big woollen mills to understand commercial production and the fibre problems involved. Her marriage brought home and children whose needs became the inspiration of her work — and led her to wool.

Wool fascinated her. She spun it appreciating the textural qualities associated with the different breeds of sheep — the fineness of Merino, the silkiness of Lincoln, the springy firmness of Drysdale and so on. She dyed it, often with natural dyes from the mulberry tree in the garden, the grey lichens on the fences or the privet berries from the hedge.

These yarns she wove and knitted into clothes for her family and furnishings for her home. Years of experiment and experience have made her familiar with many fibres both synthetic and natural — silk, cotton, mohair, angora, and dog and cow hair; because her fabrics were worn by the family and used in the house, she learnt how they should be laundered and maintained.

Today her graceful curtains of lacy wool, her rich rugs and individual upholsteries and hangings enhance many homes and institutions in Australia, such as the National University in Canberra and the Bonython Gallery in Sydney. As well, many Australians wear her elegant and hard-wearing materials. Her work has won Wool Board awards in all States, has been exhibited in many centres throughout New South Wales, and has delighted and been used by oversea designers such as Pierre Cardin.

Beryl Anderson, a practised demonstrator and teacher, has written a book that will be invaluable to textile craft students and admirers of the textile crafts. She is a member of The World Crafts Council, The Handweavers and Spinners Guild of Australia and the Craft Association of Australia.

CREATIVE SPINNING, WEAVING & PLANT-DYEING

In **Spinning, Weaving and Plant-dyeing** I have set out to give a new approach to these ancient crafts — with a simple explanation for the beginner and new methods and experiments for the more experienced craftsman.

Spinning

I have shown how to select a fleece, recognize wool qualities, distinguish different breeds, and sort, tease and card the fleece before spinning; how to make a continuous yarn on a spindle or on a spinning wheel; and how to spin yarn by the "worsted" and "woollen" methods, ply two yarns, and skein, wash, soften and dress wool. Though wool is the easiest fibre to spin, you can experiment also with cotton, silk, flax, and hair. All of these make excellent yarns. I've shown how to prepare and spin these interesting fibres.

Weaving

Detailed instructions are set out for a number of unusual weaving projects with handspun yarns, using the double weave — a method simple enough to encourage the less-experienced weaver, and provocative enough for the craftsman to produce some spectacular work. Among these projects are loom-shaped garments (a casual coat, cape poncho, and sweater), double-width fabrics without the "streak" that usually appears at the folded edges (travelling rugs, curtain fabric and a divan cover), and unusual tubular fabrics.

Plant Dyeing

Unique colours can be produced with plant dyes, and my dyeing hints and suggestions will assist you. A large table of garden plants, barks, and lichens shows the range of colours that can be extracted by using different mordants. (Before the yarns are dyed, a colour-fixative or mordant must be used; the special applications of the most common mordants are shown). A simple colour wheel illustrates the principles of colour planning and colour harmony.

Knitting Handspun

For those who knit their handspun yarn, instructions are given and suggestions for patterns, stitch gauges, blocking, and all the essentials for well-fitted garments. Knitting directions are set out (in four sizes) for a rugged ski cardigan knitted from handspun fleece.

Beryl Anderson

CREATIVE
spinning, weaving and plant-dyeing

BERYL ANDERSON

ARCO PUBLISHING COMPANY, INC.
New York

Published 1973 by Arco Publishing Company, Inc.
219 Park Avenue South, New York, N.Y. 10003

Library of Congress Catalog Card Number 72-4194

ISBN 0-668-02703-7

Printed in Singapore

CONTENTS

PHOTOGRAPHS

ABOUT THIS BOOK

A word to craftsmen by P. R. McMahon, Professor of Wool Technology and Head, School of Wool and Pastoral Sciences, The University of New South Wales.

In these days, individual progress is limited less by manual skill and acquired dexterity than by simple know-how, and the learner who wishes to advance in some of the creative crafts, is often at a loss to find someone who can demonstrate the early stages that form the basis for future progress. It is even more rare to find a Master who is able, both to teach directly and to set down simply on paper the language and techniques of a craft.

In this area those who are seeking to work with that most versatile of raw materials, the fleece of the sheep, are fortunate in having the author of the present book, Beryl Anderson. She has clearly a wide fund of knowledge and practical experience and she has set down stages of spinning and weaving with all the practical tips and hints that make achievement of beauty through colour, texture and utility, so rewarding.

In addition to working with Australia's principal natural product, wool, Beryl Anderson has experimented with other natural fibres, including a number not usually available in commercial quantities and that can be used to produce results both surprising and delightful. Perhaps her most important contribution to handcraftmanship has been her adaptation of the "complex textiles" technique of the double weave to the handloom and her exploitation of the texture potential in using demi-lustre wools with little or no twist as weft for exclusive luxury curtaining — a project only possible on the handloom. This versatility in the utilization of basically simple equipment to produce elaborate and beautiful results is the hallmark of master craftsmanship and the author is to be commended for her exposition of it.

spinning wool and other fibres

The four main breeds of sheep are — the Merino, grown for its wool, classified into super-fine, fine, medium, strong and extra-strong; the British Longwools, such as the Border Leicester, Cheviot, English Leicester, Romney Marsh and Lincoln; the Australasian breeds — Corriedale, Perendale, Poll Dorset, Polwarth, South Suffolk and Zenith; the English Shortwools — Southdown, Dorset Down, Dorset Horn, Hampshire Down, Ryeland, Shropshire and Suffolk.

Wool qualities

Wool is classed according to its fineness and length of fibre. Each type of wool is given a quality number, which mainly indicates the thickness of the wool fibre. High-quality numbers indicate very fine fibres — so when coming from 80s to 40s (see photograph) the thickness of the fibres is increasing. The length of fine wool is usually shorter than the length of coarser wools. Wool fibres have waves in them. These waves are known as crimps, and finer fibres usually have more crimps to the inch than coarser fibres.

Wool's special qualities make it an excellent fibre for spinning and weaving into garments. Wool dyes well, retains its colour, resists wrinkling, keeps its shape and tailors beautifully. It is flame resistant, long wearing, insulates against cold and heat, and absorbs moisture.

Uses of wool

Most Australian wool — used throughout the world — is especially suitable for clothing. A fleece may contain between 10 million and 50 million fibres — that grow in bundles, each more or less separate and with thousands of fibres to the bundle. Popular uses for wool include the making of many kinds of garments — from underwear to hats; and also blankets, carpets, curtains, furnishing fabrics, wall hangings and tapestries, sheepskin rugs, car-seat covers and medical sheepskins for use by hospital patients.

Selecting fleece

All wool is suitable for spinning; so the spinner should always choose fleece with characteristics that suit the articles of decoration she wishes to make. For example, you would not use a super-fine Merino, a breed outstanding for exquisitely fine-quality wool, in a floor rug. For articles that are to be walked upon and must withstand heavy wear, choose fleece with crisp, resilient fibres, that will spring back into shape when the weight is removed.

An easy wool for beginners to handle is a Crossbred with about a 48/50s count and a staple length of about 4 to 6 inches. Look for a fleece with strength and individual fibres with a reasonable crimp, without matted or cotted patches. It should be soft to handle, lustrous in appearance and have sufficient natural grease, without too much yellow yolk.

Do not neglect the fleece from the black sheep in your spinning experiments, for no longer is this sheep an outcast. It has a beautiful fleece of varying tones of light grey to charcoal, and pale fawn to deep nigger brown — that have become highly prized for natural blends in woven fabrics and good-quality knitwear.

7

Consult the wool store manager of a brokerage firm for assistance when selecting your fleeces. He is highly qualified and experienced and will guide you in your selection.

Sorting the fleece

If you are a city dweller and you buy your wool from a broker, sorting the fleece is no problem. It has already been sorted by the wool classer, and the craftsman has only to determine the breed of the sheep and the count of the wool suitable for the purpose. Here again, the advice of the store manager is helpful.

CARDING: CIRCULAR MOVEMENT WITH RIGHT HAND

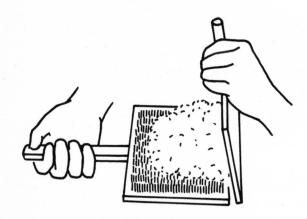

CARDING: FLICKING WOOL FREE

CARDING: ROLAG ROLLED ON BACK OF CARDER

The spinner who grows her own wool should throw the fleece out onto a large table or expanse of concrete and examine it carefully. An exceptionally good hogg fleece will be much the same all over, with only the skirtings differing noticeably. The wool growing on the legs, tail and lower haunches is coarser than the wool growing on the sides, back and shoulders. It is difficult for an inexperienced spinner to define these boundaries, but you will probably be able to see and feel the differences. Sort the fleece into bundles according to colour and texture. Each bundle should be parcelled and labelled ready for use.

Commence by removing the tail wool, hind-leg and foreleg wool. Next remove the wool of the haunches, the belly (which may be felted and rather dirty), and the under-neck wool. You now take the wool from the shoulders — the best part of the fleece — and the sides and the forward part of the back. If you can distinguish no differences in these sections, shake out any foreign matter and store the wool ready for use. Sort your black fleece in the same manner, separating the textures and the varied colours into bundles.

If your fleece has become rather dry before you have had the opportunity to sort it, lay the fleece out in the sunlight and spray it lightly (using an ordinary garden spray), with hot water. Leave it in the sun for about an hour turning it occasionally. Usually, this treatment revives the fleece, making it easy to spin.

On winter evenings, I have laid fleece to be spun, before the fire. The warmth greatly facilitates the spinning, and if you have a fleece with some heavy yolk, this method of softening is excellent. Wool is easier to spin when unwashed or "in the grease". I tease my wool in its natural greasy state before spinning.

This also enables me to take advantage of the characteristics of wool from different breeds of sheep. A really spectacular weft yarn may be spun from a Border Leicester, a fleece with a very deep crimp. For the weft yarn in an open curtain material, I have spun from the fleece without teasing. By turning the staple sideways, the crimp may be spun into loops. Since Border Leicester is a strong wool, the crimps develop an unusual twist when the fleece is spun sideways from the staple. This forms a very handsome novelty-spun yarn, in a single ply.

Teasing wool

The object of teasing, carding, flicking or combing wool (whichever method you may use), is to free and mix the fibres and incorporate as much air as possible, producing a regular yarn. To tease wool by hand, take a few staples in the left hand, holding the cut ends uppermost, and remove any vegetable matter entangled in the tips. Next, pull the fibres apart with a sideways movement. Any remaining dirt and dust should fall away.

Some spinners prefer to comb the wool before spinning, mostly using a comb from a shearing machine, that has been fitted with a small handle for easier use. Hold the staple of wool firmly by the cut ends in the left hand and pass the comb gently through the staple and out through the tips. This

Carding wool

Merino, grown for its wool classified into superfine, fine, medium, strong and extra-strong

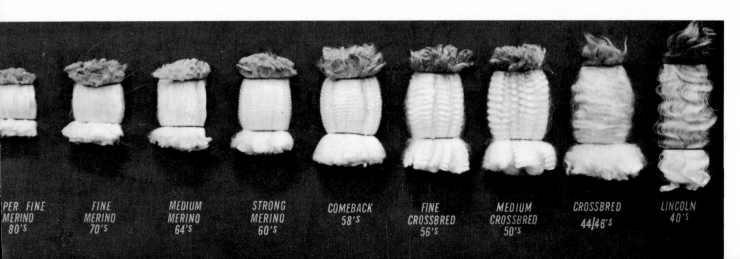

| UPPER FINE MERINO 80'S | FINE MERINO 70'S | MEDIUM MERINO 64'S | STRONG MERINO 60'S | COMEBACK 58'S | FINE CROSSBRED 56'S | MEDIUM CROSSBRED 50'S | CROSSBRED 44/46'S | LINCOLN 40'S |

Border Leicester, one of the British longwools — others are the Cheviot, English Leicester, Romney Marsh and Lincoln

Southdown, one of the English shortwools — others are the Dorset Down, Dorset Horn, Hampshire Down, Ryeland, Shropshire and Suffolk

Corriedale, one of the Australasian breeds — others are the Perendale, Poll Dorset, Polwarth, South Suffolk and Zenith

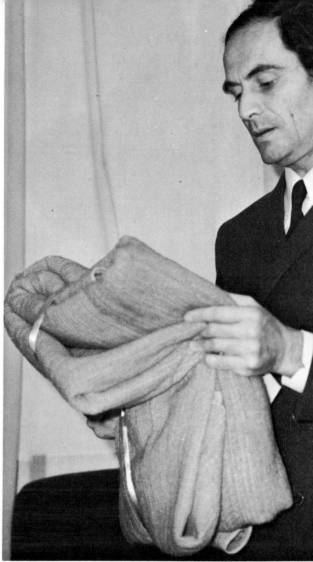

Pierre Cardin, a leading French couturier, inspects a length of handspun, handwoven fabric presented to him by the Cheviot Breeders' Society of Australia. This cloth was woven by Beryl Anderson

The shearer takes the fleece off in one piece. The fleece is then "picked up" and taken to the rolling table

Sorting fleece: after the fleece is shorn, it is laid out on a rolling table where any shabby or dirty wool is removed; the fleece is then rolled up for classing

movement removes foreign matter as well as the short woollen fibres. The woollen fibres may be saved, carded and spun later. The long worsted fibres remaining will spin into a smooth regular yarn.

A carder is a rectangular piece of wood with a handle, and measures approximately 10 X 5 inches. Rows of small wire teeth are set in leather and attached to one side. Two carders are needed for this method of preparation. First tease a small quantity of wool and remove any vegetable matter. Hold one carder in the left hand with its teeth uppermost and the handle pointing away from the body. Place a small quantity of teased wool on the carder; hold the other carder in the right hand with its teeth facing downwards and handle facing towards the body. Draw the right hand carder lightly and quickly down against the other one, two or three times and the wool will be transferred onto the right carder.

Turn the carders face to face and transfer the wool back to the left carder. Repeat this two or three times and the wool is then ready to be taken off in this manner: Hold the carders in an upright position and press the right hand carder down against the left hand one, then the left carder against the right one, flicking the wool free and transferring it to the back of the left carder. With the back of the right carder using a backwards and forwards movement roll the wool between the backs of the two carders until it is formed into a neat roll, called a "rolag". It is now ready for spinning.

I think the fastest and most satisfactory method of teasing wool is with a "flicker", a miniature carder. It is a light, rectangular-shaped piece of wood measuring approximately 4 X 2½ inches, with a handle and rows of small wire teeth set in leather, on one surface as on a carder. Only one flicker is necessary. Take a staple in the left hand, grasping the cut ends firmly between the fingers and thumb. Holding the flicker in the right hand, teeth facing downwards, firmly flick the tips of the staple with a quick, light movement. The fibres separate, throwing out any foreign matter entangled in the tips. If necessary, turn the staple and flick the cut ends. There is no waste with this method. The wool is now ready for spinning.

When it is necessary to prepare a large quantity of wool, a carding machine is desirable (see colour photo). The fleece must be washed and teased before being put through the machine. The wool is placed on the tray and fed under the small-toothed roller. The carded wool collects on the large drum. A carding machine is also useful for colour blending wool. The machine is operated by a small handle on the side — or it can easily be motorized by a handyman.

Making a continuous yarn

The spindle

The oldest method of producing a continuous yarn is with a spindle. The spindle was once simply a stick with a hook on one end. From the Aztec civilization surviving relics show an interesting traditional design. The spindle is a slender wooden stick ten to twelve inches in length and balanced at the lower end by a pottery whorl.

This is the simplest form of spinning known and consists of three processes: forming a thread by drawing fibres out; twisting threads for strength; and winding the spun yarn. Other simple methods are spinning with the hands alone and spinning with hand and thigh. Spinning with the hands alone is slow, for the three processes (drawing out or drafting, twisting, and winding) are done separately.

When spinning on the thigh, the thread is rolled on the thigh with one hand, while the other draws the thread — which is produced more quickly.

For spinners who wish to try spinning with a spindle, here are a few directions: The spindle is a slender wooden stick about 12 inches long with a hook at one end and a point at the other. A wooden disc, called a whorl, is fitted to the stick about an inch above the point, to help the spindle balance and revolve easily.

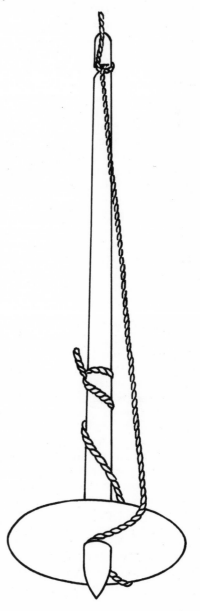

Wool tied to the spindle

9

A length of about 12 inches of handspun or machine wool is needed to form a leader thread. Tie the end of the wool to the spindle just above the whorl. Pass it over the whorl, round the stem below it, up again from here to the top of the stem and loop it round the hook, with a half-hitch knot to hold it securely. Hold the teased wool lightly in the left hand and draw out a length of about 4 inches, that will give the required thickness of the yarn when it is twisted. Overlap the ends of the new thread and the leader thread and hold them between the left finger and thumb. With the right hand twist the spindle sharply to the right, as if twisting a top, and let it spin until there is a tight twist on the leader thread. Ease the left finger and thumb away from the joining point and let the twist run along so that the two ends are fastened together.

When the twist reaches the end of the 4-inch length of wool drawn from the fleece, hold the wool at this point between the finger and thumb of the right hand, and draw out another length of the same thickness from your teased wool. Remove the fingers and let the twist run along again. When all the twist is used, hold the finishing point with the left-hand finger and thumb and repeat the process by twisting the spindle again.

The skill lies in teasing the fleece well and handling it deftly and lightly — this enables you to keep the spindle rotating. With a little practice, you can become quite proficient at using a spindle. Next wind the length of spun yarn onto the stem of the spindle just above the whorl. To do this, slip the yarn from the notch at the top; then wind it onto the stem of the spindle, as though winding a cone of wool. Wind it crosswise up and down the spindle, allowing each layer to come a little higher so that, when the spindle is full, the yarn will be wound into a cone. Leave enough wool unwound to hitch it to the spindle, and repeat this process until the stem is sufficiently full. Slip the cone shape off the spindle (it will slip off quite easily) and place it on a stand made from fine dowel rods, until ready for use.

The spinning wheel

Spinning on a wheel has captured the imagination of man throughout the ages and today it is one of the most popular handcrafts. The spinning wheel is the only machine on which it is possible, without any special adjustments, to spin wool, cotton, hairs, flax or silk. The most exciting thing about spinning your own yarn is that you can design and govern the appearance of the finished article — whether knitted or handwoven.

There are three basic systems of spinning with a wheel — the system of using an upright wheel; the system of spinning with a double-driving band, producing a positive drive upon both the spindle and bobbin (as is found in the Pipy wheel); and the system of using a positive drive upon the spindle and a braking action on the bobbin (as in the Ashford wheel).

Before commencing to spin on your wheel, study it carefully and familiarize yourself with its particular system of spinning. Before attempting to spin your yarn, it is most important that you have complete control of the wheel's motion with your foot. If this is mastered in the beginning,

one of the spinner's greatest problems, "overtwist", will be avoided.

First place the crank of the wheel off-centre to the right in a 5 past 12 position. If the crank stands immediately upright, no matter how hard you press on the pedal you cannot move it. Balance the wheel by revolving it slightly first in a clockwise direction, then in an anti-clockwise direction, by using a toe heel motion with your foot. Revolve the wheel to the right by pressing gently down with your toes, then down with the heel to bring it back to the left. Practise this balancing movement first, for it will quickly enable you to gain the feel of the wheel.

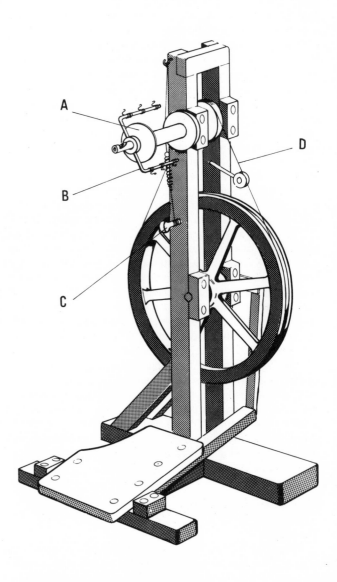

Upright wheel: "A" bobbin; "B" flyer; "C" bobbin tension screw; "D" single drive band

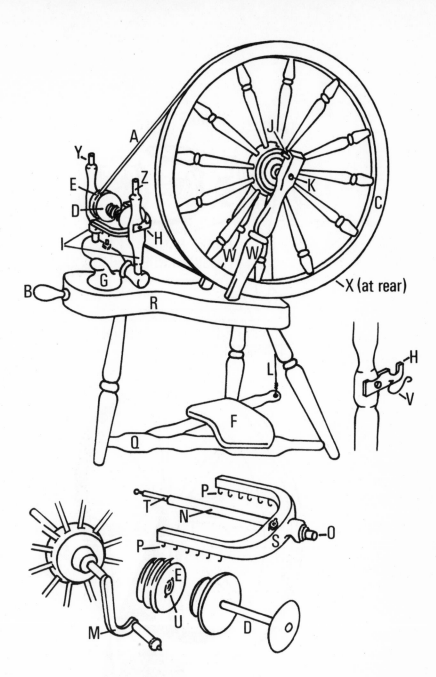

Pipy wheel: a positive drive on both spindle and bobbin. Double driving band

"A" double driving band; "B" tension screw; "C" wheel; "D" bobbin; "E" spindle whorl; "F" treadle; "G" mother-of-all; "H" metal bearings; "I" maidens; "J" wheel pegs; "K" axle bearings; "L" treadle cord; "M" axle crank; "N" spindle shaft; "O" orifice; "P" guide hooks; "Q" treadle bar; "R" table; "S" flyer; "T" spline; "U" key way; "V" rapid flyer release; "W" uprights; "X" wheel balance; "Y" mounting for distaff; "Z" mounting for lamp

When you are able to control the wheel, set the crank off-centre to the right, and make one full revolution of the wheel, bringing the crank back to its original position. A sharp thrust downward with the toes will set it in motion, then thrust downward with the heel to hold it stationary in its original position.

Make every revolution of the wheel work for you. One full revolution of a wheel, approximately 21½ inches in diameter, will pull in about 3 inches of wool onto the bobbin. The amount pulled in will vary according to the size of the wheel. Only when you are proficient at these movements and are able to control your wheel, can you begin to make a thread.

Spinning the yarn

Twisting is the important factor in spinning. All fibres have irregularities (visible under a microscope) — wool fibres have a unique structure similar to scales, cotton fibres have kinks and twists, and flax fibres have knots. By means of these irregularities the fibres cling together when twisted. The twisting therefore gives elasticity and strength to the spun yarn.

The main aim of the spinner is to produce a yarn that suits the task of the fabric. Yarns used for knitting need a softer twist than those used for weaving a hard-wearing top-coat. A warp yarn to be used in a piece of woven material, will need more twist than a yarn used in the weft.

Yarns spun when a spindle or spinning wheel is revolving in a clockwise direction are known as Z-twisted, while yarns spun in an anti-clockwise direction are known as S-twisted. Each type of wool must be studied individually and handled

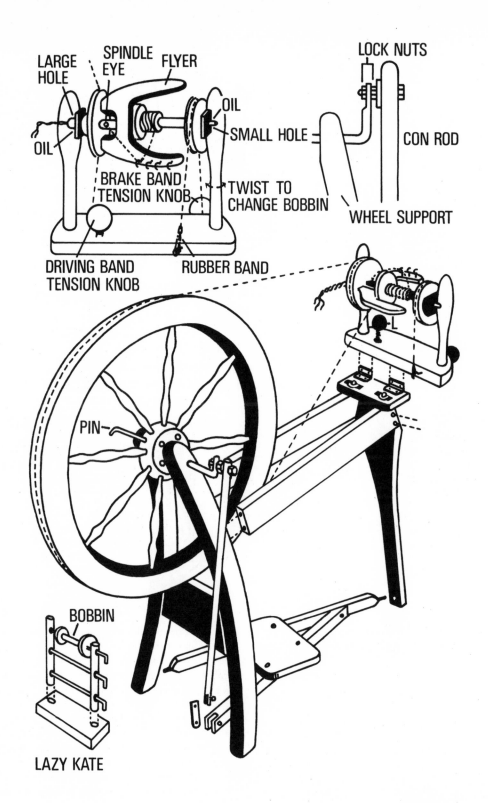

LARGE HOLE

SPINDLE EYE

FLYER

OIL

OIL

SMALL HOLE

BRAKE BAND TENSION KNOB

TWIST TO CHANGE BOBBIN

DRIVING BAND TENSION KNOB

RUBBER BAND

LOCK NUTS

CON ROD

WHEEL SUPPORT

PIN

BOBBIN

LAZY KATE

Ashford wheel: a positive drive on the spindle and a braking action on the bobbin

accordingly. Most craftsmen spin short-stapled fleece by the "woollen" method. This involves mixing short fine wools until they are soft and of even density, incorporating as much air as possible, and forming a hollow tube known as a rolag.

The "worsted" method is particularly suitable for long-stapled lustrous wools. Worsted spinning, comes about when the long fibres lie parallel as the twist runs in; this makes a smooth yarn that is firmer and less hairy than a woollen yarn. Almost any type of fleece can be spun by the worsted method, but a long-stapled fleece is best suited to this.

Take a lock of wool by the cut ends and, using a comb from a shearing machine, draw it through the length of the staple. Next take the lock by the tips and draw the comb out through the cut ends. The short woollen fibres, that have accumulated in the comb are called "noils", and may be saved to card and spin later. The long or "worsted" fibres will remain straight and parallel in the hand, ready for spinning. Part the fibres at the cut ends, draw out and commence to spin.

Holding the prepared staple by the tips in the left hand, pull a few fibres apart with a sideways motion, then pull them forward towards the bobbin until you have drawn out approximately 3 inches. Hold the staple lightly, and as you draw the wool forward, the fibres will glide easily in the natural grease — if handled deftly.

Take the drawn-out fibres and wrap them round the end of the leader thread. Hold the join between the finger and thumb of the left hand. Make one full revolution with the wheel, returning the crank to the off-centre position. This will allow the twist made on the wool to run up the join and secure it; make another full revolution of the wheel allowing the thread to feed onto the bobbin. Hold the thread between the right finger and thumb in front of the orifice of the spindle, and draw back the staple with the left hand until you have a length of about 3 inches. Take the right hand away, and make one full revolution with the wheel, allowing the length to run forward onto the bobbin.

Repeat the process in this order: set the crank of the wheel off-centre to the right; determine the yarn size (thickness and length); and make one full revolution of the wheel allowing the yarn to run onto the bobbin.

I have found that teaching a student to understand the foot movement and master these three actions — holding the wheel in a stationary position; determining the yarn size; allowing the required amount of yarn to feed onto the bobbin — often enables him to synchronize quickly and easily the movement of drawing out the fibres and transmitting motion to the wheel. He will also become aware of the problem of overtwist, and learn how this can be prevented.

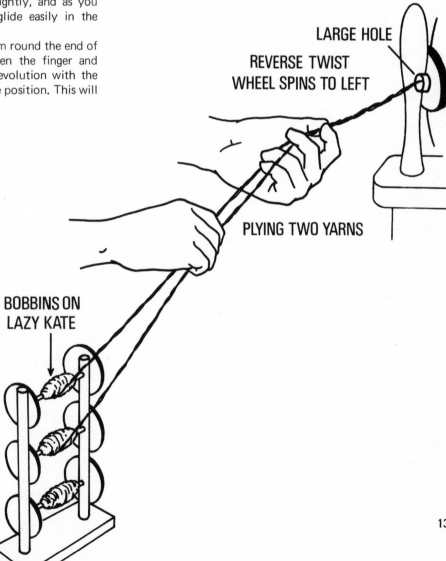

LARGE HOLE

REVERSE TWIST
WHEEL SPINS TO LEFT

PLYING TWO YARNS

BOBBINS ON
LAZY KATE

Plying two yarns

This not only eliminates one of the spinner's greatest obstacles, but also encourages him to experiment with different yarns and make ones suitable for his particular project. For example, if a fine even yarn is required pull only a few fibres out of the staple. If producing a slub yarn, turn the staple sideways and pinch out a tuft. As confidence is gained, the student will be able to produce the required yarn on a steadily rotating wheel.

Plying two yarns

To make a two-ply wool: two strands of single yarn are twisted together, with the wheel revolving to the left. If you take a length of Z-twisted yarn and fold it back on itself, you will notice that the two ends of the yarn will twist together in a direction opposite to the twist of the single yarn — two S-twisted singles will ply into a Z-twist.

The simplest two-ply is made by twisting together two Z-twisted singles using an S-twist. Place an empty bobbin on the spindle, and draw a leader thread through the eye of the spindle ready for spinning. Place two filled bobbins onto the creel, or bobbin holder, and tie the ends to the leader thread. Stand the bobbin holder by your left side. Revolve the wheel slowly to the left until the knot is past the distribution hooks.

Separate the two yarns with the right forefinger and control the feed-in with the left hand. You may find it simpler to hold the yarns separately in both hands, and so have more control over the number of twists to the inch being spun into the plied yarn.

More brakehand tension is required for plying; and the tension is gradually increased as the bobbin fills. Faster treadling is also necessary, and the wool must be fed in smoothly. If the wool is jerked from the bobbin-holder it will cause tangles and back-lash. Practice is necessary to produce a really good plied yarn, and erratic treadling will cause uneven work.

Whether spinning with a wheel or spindle there are a great variety of uses for the yarn and many opportunities for design with both single and plied yarns. Very interesting two-ply yarns may be made by varying the characteristics of the two single yarns. For example, spin the wool in a soft, slub manner using an S-twist. Ply it with a mill-spun, fine worsted yarn that has been Z-twisted. Ply these two yarns together with a Z-twist to make an unusual yarn. A slub yarn — another interesting variation — is made by turning the staple sideways when spinning and pinching out tufts, instead of drawing it out smoothly.

Experiment by exerting more pressure on the fine worsted yarn, or by using silk thread instead of the worsted yarn. Two coloured yarns, natural brown and white, spun in a slub manner and plied lightly together with an S-twist, will make an elegant yarn for knitting ski-wear. Experiment with your favourite colour combinations in this way, or bind coloured wools together on the carders and spin from the rolag.

Another interesting experiment is made by placing a fine layer of wool in the left carder and sprinkling it with bright, left-over, mill-spun knitting yarns that have been snipped into small pieces, before carding in the usual way. The results are both surprising and beautiful. Experiment also by plying and by making other fancy yarns.

Skeining and washing the wool

Release the brakehand tension and wind the wool into skeins round a "swift" or wool skeiner. Tie the skeins loosely in three places to prevent ravelling.

They are now ready to be washed. Place the wool in a sink under running water, where it is possible to regulate the heat of the water. Squeeze the wool gently and remove as much loose dirt as possible. The temperature of the water should always be warm; if it is too hot the yarn will mat and stick together. Lie it on the sink, cover with warm water, and sprinkle with a safe, efficient wool washing powder. Squeeze the soap powder gently into each skein, working up a good lather. Let it soak for about half an hour if the fleece is very dirty, and repeat the process if necessary. When the skeins are clean, rinse them thoroughly under running water until all soap is removed. (I lie them over the agitator centre of the washing machine and spin the water out). Shake the skeins well to separate the strands, then place them on a cord over the clothes line and leave them to dry. It is advisable to shake the skeins from time to time; this frees the strands and helps the wool to dry soft and fluffy.

To soften a harsh wool

Not very long ago, sweet oil and soda, borax, and carbonate of potash were used for softening harsh wool. These were not completely successful, especially when the wool was dyed afterwards. It is now possible to buy a highly effective commercial softener that may be used on skeined wool, or on dyed woven fabric. This is called Sapamine WL, produced by the C.I.B.A. Company. It is suitable for all types of fibres and doesn't affect shade or light fastness of the dyes. It is a whitish paste and is diluted by stirring the same amount, by weight, of boiling water and then boiling. This mixture is then further diluted with eight times its amount of hot water, and boiled again for a short time.

Dressing wool

If fleece is very dirty, making it necessary to wash the wool before spinning, it is essential to work a good dressing oil into the fleece before commencing to spin. Make a mixture of 1 part olive oil, ½ part water, ¼ part ammonia and heat the mixture in a saucepan. Spread the fleece out on an old sheet. Pour the heated mixture into a garden spray, spray the fleece lightly all over. Knead the mixture into the fleece. It may be necessary to spray the fleece two or three times. Roll the fleece up in the sheet and leave for several days before spinning. The fibres will glide quite easily when spun.

Spinning other fibres

Wool is the easiest fibre to spin, because of its special structure, though yarns can also be spun from other fibres. Cottons, silks, hairs or flax make exquisite yarns.

Cotton

Cotton is another excellent raw material for spinning. The cotton plant grows from two to six feet high with spreading branches that gradually become shorter towards the top. After flowering, green bolls appear. The boll is the seed pod of the cotton plant, and contains many dark seeds closely wrapped in cotton fibres. The boll grows to about the size of a walnut and, as it ripens, turns brown in colour and opens slowly. The cotton fibres burst from the boll like white snowballs.

The cotton fibres are firmly attached to the seeds and, for the spinner who grows his own cotton, the easiest way to remove the seeds is to place a handful of fibres into a colander and steam them over a saucepan of boiling water for a few minutes. Lift the fibres apart with a long skewer as they commence to rise, and the fluffy mass of cotton will be easy to handle and spin. Do not steam for too long. The fibres should not become wet.

I also use this method to separate the fibres of the wide bands of compressed cotton that comes from the mill. Raw cotton from the mill varies considerably in length of staple, freedom from vegetable matter, and in colour. Cotton fibres have microscopic kinks and twists and, by means of these irregularities, the fibres cling together when spun.

When spinning cotton on the wheel, only a light tension is needed on the brake band. Hold the steamed cotton in the left hand and draw out the fibres with a slight untwisting movement of the right thumb along the forefinger to make it easier to control. With a little practice you can spin the yarn of your choice. The main difficulty in spinning short fibres is to adapt the short quick draw to the rate of treadling and the speed of·winding on. The yarn may be rather tightly twisted at first, but the spinner can adjust this when he has learned to control the fibres.

An even yarn is rather difficult to spin, but the texture of the processed cotton lends itself well to novelty spinning. A slub type yarn can be most attractive, and cotton plied with various fine yarns gives an interesting texture.

Flax

The preparation of flax fibres for spinning is long and arduous and, as many books have been written on this, I will describe only the method of spinning dressed fibres. It is necessary to assemble the long fibres so that they may be drawn out without tangling and causing wastage of material. A bundle of flax is called a "strick", and experienced spinners prefer to fold the fibres into a cone shape and tie them onto a distaff attached to the spinning wheel. In countries where flax is readily obtainable, it is common to see a small bowl set into the table of the spinning wheel, to enable the craftsman to keep his forefinger and thumb damp when drawing fibres from the distaff.

Many spinners use the following method to fold the flax before tying to the distaff: Take about 2 yards of soft ribbon about ½ inch wide and a length of string. Place a cloth on a table. Tie the string firmly to the strick of flax about 3 inches from the end, and tie the ends round your waist. Place the

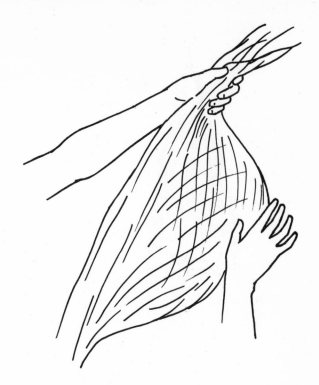

Flax spinning: with your right hand, separate a few fibres from the strick and hold them on the table with the palm of the hand

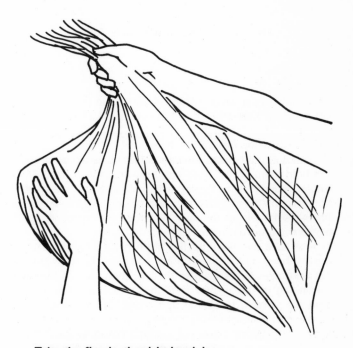

Take the flax in the right hand, lay the palm of the left hand on the film of fibres, and draw the strick back to the right, to make a "fan shape"

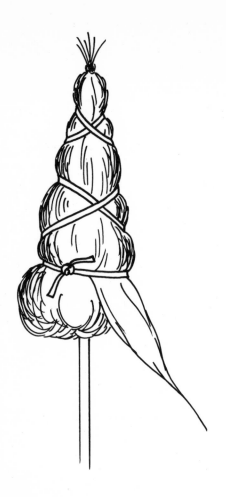

Flax tied to the distaff ready for spinning

Before folding the flax onto the distaff it should first be covered with tissue paper. Place a couple of sheets of tissue on the table and roll the distaff across them diagonally. Neaten the fold. This assists to hold the flax in position. Lay the distaff on the right-hand edge of the fan with the top close to the knot. Remove the knot then roll the distaff into the fan shape. Smooth the join down gently and set the distaff in the holder. Tie the centre of the ribbon round the top of the distaff, where formerly the knot had been tied, with a fairly tight single knot and cross the ribbon about the cone shape several times, tying securely at the lower edge. Tidy the distaff by tucking up any loose ends.

The flax is now ready to spin. Place the distaff to the left, slightly in front of the orifice of the spindle. With a damp finger and thumb, draw down a few fibres from the bottom of the distaff and twist them onto the leader thread. Treadle slowly, gently drawing the fibres down with the left hand using a slight twisting movement of forefinger and thumb. As the flax on the distaff becomes less the ribbon should be retied. With a little practice, the spinner can quickly adjust to spinning flax.

Short flax fibres that have been combed, or "hackled" from the strick are called "tow"; the long flax fibres are called "line". Good flax spinning depends almost entirely on the care with which the distaff is dressed.

Silk

One of the best forms of silk for the handspinner is "frisson". It resembles untidy bundles of straw, and is strong and very gummy. To prepare the silk for spinning it is necessary first to remove the gum from the bundles. Prepare a solution of Lux and water and simmer the bundles in this mixture for a couple of hours. Then rinse the silk in hot water and again simmer in a fresh bath of Lux and water. The soap solution dissolves the gum with which the silk is coated. Rinse again in hot water and hang out to dry. The filaments are then cut into four-inch lengths, combed on a carder, and spun.

It is quite easy to spin silk, as one becomes accustomed to the feel. A very successful slub yarn can be spun from silk. The raw silk dress (see colour photo), was woven using a slub yarn in both warp and weft.

Angora rabbit hair

The length of staple of the Angora rabbit hair I use for spinning is about 3 inches. I have found it quite difficult to spin at first, since the fibres are fine and slippery. It is necessary to move the hands very quickly in relation to the rate of treadling as the amount drawn out at one time is very small. The rabbit hair is spun the same way as a worsted yarn, but it is not necessary to comb the fibres before spinning.

Another interesting experiment is made by carding the hair with a small amount of fine wool. Place a layer of wool on the left carder, with a layer of hair on top and card in the usual manner. (I have knitted this yarn into a very comfortable cardigan.) Angora hair easily accepts both commercial and plant dyes.

strick out on the table in front of you. Take the flax in your left hand, as near the far end as you can reach, and keeping your left arm outstretched, move it over to the right — the objective being to make a fan shape.

With the right hand, separate a few fibres from the strick and hold them on the table with the palm of your hand. Move the left hand over to the left side, pulling out a fine layer of fibres as you do so. Place the palm of your right hand on the fibres on the left, at the same time raise the left hand a little higher and draw out more fibres.

Now take the flax into the right hand and lay the palm of the left hand on the film of fibres, and draw the strick back to the right side. Cross again to the left, then back to the right, continuing in this manner until the strick is used up. As you draw the fibres from side to side, do not allow any to lie as if radiating in a straight line (at right angles) from where the flax is tied. Usually the fibres pull out in a crosswise form; this is necessary to produce a well-dressed distaff that will not disintegrate when the fibres are pulled downwards when spinning. Untie the string from your waist, gently loosen the fibres round the knot and fold over any loose ends round the bottom of the fan.

Shorthorn cow hair

I have found cow hair the most difficult fibre to spin. The hair is short (about ¼ inch in length), hard and slippery. On the wheel, the leader thread must be wool. Lay the leader thread on the bundle of cut hair and observe how the short fibres twist. (I must confess that when experimenting with cowhair, the yarn I spun was very tightly twisted and resembled tinsel in appearance. It was later woven successfully into a novelty wall hanging. A further experiment using a combination of broad wool with the hair was easier to spin.)

Dog combings

The combings or clippings from long-haired dogs such as Afghan, Poodle, Collie or Samoyed spin into beautiful yarns similar to Cashmere in quality. They may be plied together or with other yarns according to the kind of article to be made. Dog clippings make excellent knitting yarns.

Mohair

Mohair is the fine long lustrous fibre from the Angora goat. It may be spun by the worsted method into fine yarns, or advantage taken of the deep crimp to produce beautiful novelty yarns. In worsted spinning the fibres lie parallel as the twist runs in.

To prepare and spin the mohair, consider the article you wish to make, the design and the texture you want, and the condition of the fleece you will use. If you have kept the fleece for some time, and it has become matted and rather dry, lay it on a piece of paper in the sunlight and gently tease it apart with your fingers.

Make a mixture of 1 part olive oil, ½ part water and ¼ part ammonia. Warm the mixture, pour into a garden spray, and lightly spray the teased fleece. Leave it in the sun for about half an hour, then roll it up in the paper and leave it for several days. After this, the long fibres may be flicked, or combed, and spun in the worsted manner. If the fibres do not appear to be satisfactory for this treatment they may be carded together with a suitable wool.

Place a fine layer of wool on the left carder — enough to enable you to bind the mohair together. Instead of making a rolag, roll the mohair-wool mixture by hand from left to right across the carder; it is now ready for spinning.

To prepare mohair for spinning by the worsted method, I prefer to use a flicker, as this instrument does not damage the fibres or waste the mohair. To spin, hold the staple by the tips in the left hand. With the right hand, gently pull a few fibres apart sideways, then pull forward towards the leader yarn in the spinning wheel. The secret of handling mohair is to hold the staple lightly so that the fibres glide easily as they are drawn.

Exquisite novelty yarns may be spun by turning the staple sideways and spinning slub effects. Mohair yarns can be plied together or with other yarns, whether spun evenly or in a novelty fashion. Mohair also dyes beautifully. If the fleece is first grade, it requires little preparation before it is dyed. Soak it overnight in warm water and press all water out before putting it in the dye bath.

Very dirty fleece may require a careful rinsing in a safe efficient wool washing powder and warm water, before being left to soak overnight. Any recipe for dyeing wool, whether with a commercial dye or a plant material, may be successfully used with mohair. Because of its structure, articles made from mohair fibres are crease-resistant.

weaving
with spun and unspun wool

The projects described here make use of the double weave, which is simple enough to encourage the beginner weaver to experiment and provocative enough for the craftsman to produce some spectacular work. This extremely versatile weave offers endless possibilities for design. The double cloth, tubular and double-width fabrics, of either plain or patterned design can be woven from a simple threading on a four-shaft loom.

Of these projects, the loom-designed garments, the curtain fabrics, bedspread and double-woven, double-width travelling rug were all woven on four shafts with a twill threading. I have emphasized the weaving of a double-width fabric without "streak", which usually appears at the folded edges of articles. I have also shown the weaving of two independent fabrics simultaneously to produce loom-shaped articles, which require a minimum of finishing, after they have been woven and removed from the loom.

The success of these contemporary-styled articles depends on the attention paid to a few simple details: Plan the exact shape of the garment on graph paper, with one square representing one inch. The shape is woven by inserting and withdrawing the shuttle in the body of the design to form selvedges, where the cut edges would be if the material were yardage. Allow adequate material for take up and shrinkage.

When an unspun wool is used in the weft, a strong warp yarn is required — it may be widely spaced, to show to advantage the beauty of a particular fleece. Do not place too strong a tension on the warp yarn — for this will cause excessive take-up when the tension is relaxed.

One problem that occurs when weaving shaped garments is that when certain areas of the warp are left unwoven, the threads in these parts tend to sag because there is no take-up from the weft. I have discovered that the easiest way to overcome this is to insert a row of heavy cotton wool bandage at intervals to prevent the unwoven sections from becoming soft, and to avoid tension problems when the weaving of the full warp is resumed. The bandage is easily removed when the garment is cut from the loom. Ideally, when planning the design, these sections could be used for sampling or for making accessories, for most weavers dislike wasting any part of a warp.

Tie-up

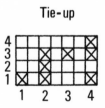

Threading

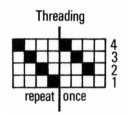

repeat | once

Treadling Orders

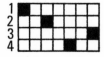

For weaving double-width fabric. Denting: one per dent, miss one dent, two per dent across body of the warp

18

Casual coat

This coat (see colour photo), is woven with the fold down the centre line. Using two shuttles, weave the hems on both pieces with the same material as the warp. From the lower edge to the sleeve shaping is twenty-five inches. Weave for five inches, then make the shaping for the front neck-line. Weave four inches, then the fold line for the shoulders is reached. Weave one inch farther — this allows for shaping the back neck-line.

Change to one shuttle and weave the back section according to the diagram. The weaver quickly adjusts to the tension required to eliminate the fold-line down the centre-back of the garment. When the coat is removed from the loom, cut the warp threads about three inches on either side of the sleeves and knot the yarns together to form the sleeve seams. Cut and knot the neck edges in a similar manner. The yarns are then darned back into the material to form a neat edge. Turn up the lower edges and hem. Sew the side seams. A decorative edge may be made at the side simply by placing both edges together.

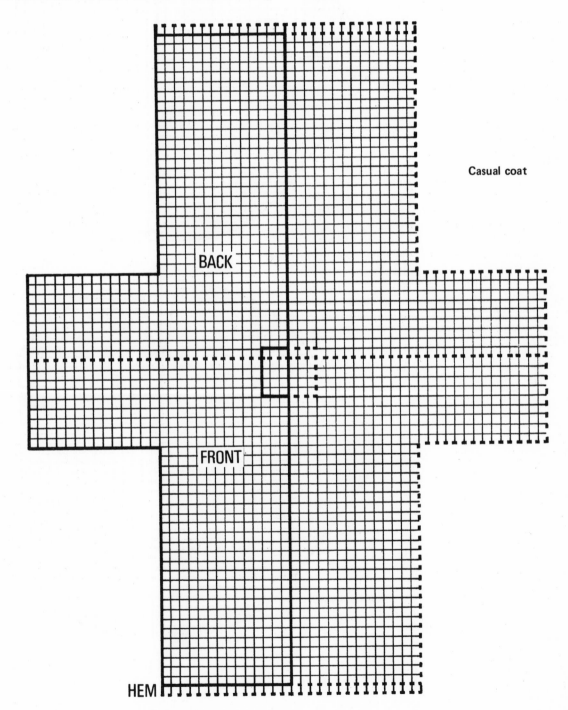

Casual coat

BACK

FRONT

HEM

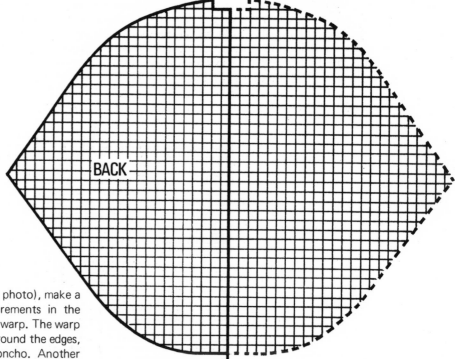

Cape poncho

Before weaving the cape poncho (see colour photo), make a pattern, cut it out according to the measurements in the diagram, and use it to mark the shape on the warp. The warp fringes are knotted over the shoulder-line and round the edges, then darned back into the body of the poncho. Another attractive garment can be made with the shoulder fringes tied and left on the outside. The fringed edges are made with handspun wool. Several lengths are cut and doubled in the centre. The loop thus formed is drawn through the selvedge, both ends are then drawn through the loop and tightened. A long scarf can be knitted by hand with spun wool and attached to the back neck-line.

Cape poncho

Sweater

This sweater (see colour photo), is woven with handspun wool from a Corriedale fleece, incorporating both natural and coloured wool, using the double-width method of weaving.

In making the sweater the centre line is retained and used in a decorative manner. Commencing at the lower front edge and weaving with two shuttles, the yarns are interlocked at the fold-line and woven in this way until the neck shaping is reached. From this point, where the widening of the sleeves occurs, the natural Corriedale yarn is used.

The fringed warp ends can be turned under to give the sweater a more tailored appearance. The warp fringes can be left outside on the sleeve seams and the lower edge. The neck is finished in the same way for each sweater. This sweater, like the cape poncho and the casual coat, can be adapted to fit a man, and makes very handsome ski-wear. These garments, with softly draped lines, can be worn with flare by any figure size.

Sweater

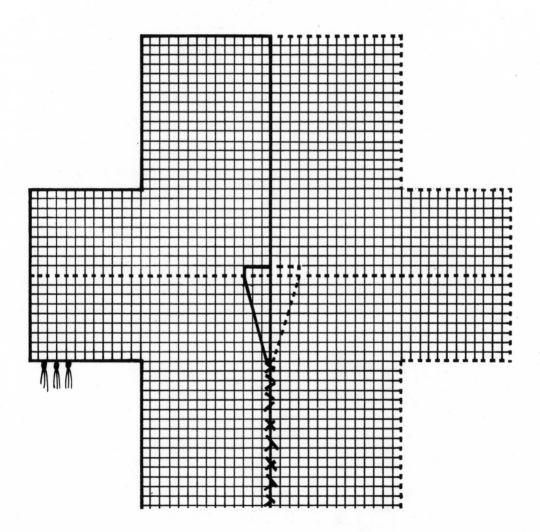

Double-width curtain fabric and divan cover
Curtain fabric (see colour photo)
Warp: yellow and gold wool loop

Weft: brilliant yellow, plant-dyed, handspun Border Leicester fleece. Ends per inch: 12. Reed: 15 dent. Fold on the right-hand side. Thread singly in heddles.

Denting:

1 per dent
1 empty dent
2 per dent
2 empty dents
2 per dent for 2 dents
(Thread once only)
* 4 empty dents
2 per dent for 2 dents
1 empty dent
2 per dent for 3 dents
1 empty dent
2 per dent for 2 dents
1 empty dent
2 per dent for 3 dents
4 empty dents
2 per dent for 2 dents
4 empty dents
2 per dent for 2 dents
4 empty dents
2 per dent for 3 dents
4 empty dents
2 per dent for 2 dents
1 empty dent
2 per dent for 3 dents
1 empty dent
2 per dent for 2 dents
Repeat from * for desired width.

Divan cover (see colour photo)
Threading and treadling orders are the same as given for the double-width curtain. The weft is also Border Leicester. Dyed in the fleece and colour-blended, the wool is carded and laid in the shed by "finger weaving".

Threading

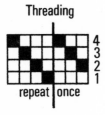

repeat | once

Tie-up

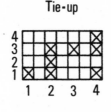

Treadling Orders

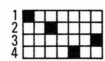

For weaving double-width curtain fabric and divan cover

Sun-room curtains
These sun-room curtains (see colour photo), of a comparatively low-cost design, are sufficiently translucent to allow the maximum of light at all times and heavy enough to drape gracefully and protect from the sun's rays when needed. The curtains could be excellent for entirely curtaining a sun-room.

The warp arrangement is a two-inch opaque stripe repeat of wool loop and a two-inch mesh. Warp: wool loop. Weft: wool loop and handspun. Reed: 6 dent.

Tie-up   ### Threading

Treadling Orders

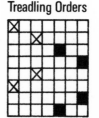

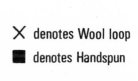

X denotes Wool loop

■ denotes Handspun

For weaving sun-room curtains.
Denting: remove thread from shaft 1
and discard.
1 per dent
1 empty dent
2 per dent for 14 dents
(Thread once only)

16 empty dents
2 per dent for 16 dents
(Repeat for desired width)

Fold on right-hand side

Cushion from tubular fabric
(see colour photo)
For tubular pattern, omit the first and second threads of the first repeat of the twill threading, and treadle: 1, 3, 2, 4 and repeat. Treadle 5 and 6 alternately, to weave a single fabric, forming a frill at the end. Weave tubing for the length of the pillow. Separate the two fabrics by treadling 1 and 2

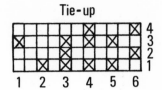

Tie-up

Threading

together and insert the pillow. Weave 5 and 6 alternately to weave the pillow in and form the frill at the end.

If desired, the edges may be woven in double width. The fabric thus formed may be turned in and the folded edges whipped together, or the ends may be finished with a fringe by knotting the warp threads.

The materials used for the cushion in the photograph are as follows:
Warp: 2/18s worsted
Weft: handspun and unspun wool
Reed: 10 dent
Denting: 2 per dent.

Travelling rug

The travelling rug offers endless possibilities for design. The warp may consist of a combination of yarns of varying textures and colours and the weft of handspun, lustrous wools. Sensitively woven in natural materials with an inherent beauty, the rug is both functional and attractive and provides the weaver with one of the most satisfying pieces of craft work that can be created from the loom.

The rug in my most recent project on the double-weave theme (see colour photograph), was woven with a combination of nubbly handspun and fine tweed yarns.
Warp: fine tweed and handspun
Weft: fine tweed and handspun
Ends per inch: 10
Thread singly in heddles
Reed: 10 dent
Thread 1 handspun and 1 tweed yarn together, per dent
Fold on the right-hand side.

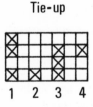

Tie-up

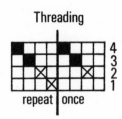

Threading

repeat | once

Treadling Orders

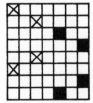

× denotes Tweed yarn

■ denotes Handspun

Denting: one tweed yarn, one empty dent, one tweed yarn, plus one handspun per dent, across body of the warp

There are countless possibilities for using the double weave — I have provided only a few examples to guide the weaver in his experiments.

Quexquemetl

The Quexquemetl (pronounced ketch-kem-etal), is the Mexican version of the poncho. This delightfully zany garment may be woven in an evening and makes a very acceptable gift. Light and particularly warm, the quexquemetl makes a gorgeously colour-harmonized cover-up. This popular contemporary version of the old fashioned stole, enables the weaver to use the small amounts of beautiful, textured yarns left over in his store-cupboard.

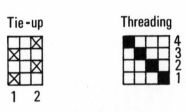

Tie-up   Threading

Treadle: 1, 2, alternately

For weaving quexquemetl

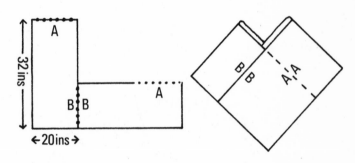

The fun piece (see colour photo), was woven on a four-shaft loom, with a straight twill threading. The materials and directions are:
Warp: wool boucle
Weft: unspun Crossbred
Threads per inch: 6
Reed: 6 dent
Denting: 1 per dent.

Weave two rectangular pieces, thirty-two by twenty inches, or the size required. Join as shown in the diagram. The decorative fringe is simply a continuation of the unspun weft. If this is not desired, the edges may be neatly hemmed, or the tassels hooked and tied round the entire outer edge.

23

plant-dyeing

unspun fleece or handspun yarn

The colour wheel

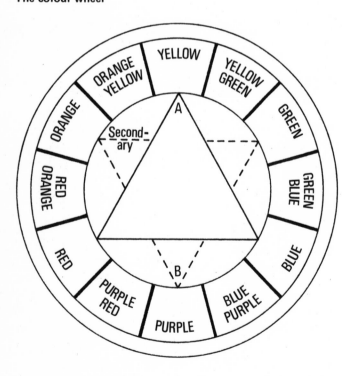

The majority of craftsmen, after learning how to spin their own yarn, naturally seek a means of introducing colour to their art. Dyeing is a craft in itself, whether with a commercial product or with plant material.

Excellent commercial dyes are produced by the I.C.I. and other companies. They are by no means difficult to handle, but success depends on the selection of the correct dye for a specific fibre and following the manufacturer's instructions most carefully.

Colour planning made easy

The colour wheel has proved to be a most reliable basis for producing harmonious colour schemes. Many complicated colour circles have been devised within the various colour systems, but the one shown here is simple and practical.

To make your own colour selection, cut out triangle "A" and rotate it on a centre pin. Choose one colour to dominate; use the other two colours as accessories. The triangles "A" and "B" show the primary colours, red, blue and yellow with their complementary colours opposite and the secondary colours obtained from a mixture of two primaries. For example, the complement of the colour red is green, obtained from mixing the two remaining primary colours, blue and yellow. This principle applies to all colours in the wheel.

The principles used to obtain a harmonious colour scheme in adding colour to handspun yarns in this exciting field of design are shown in the colour harmony diagrams.

Spinning Cheviot wool for weaving upholstery fabric, on a Norwegian wheel. The soft furnishings — rug and chair covers — are woven from Cheviot fleece

Flicking wool: take a staple in the left hand, grasping the cut ends firmly between the fingers and thumb. Hold the flicker in the right hand, teeth facing downwards. Firmly flick the tips of the staple with a quick, light movement

Determine the yarn size (thickness and length): hold the thread between the right finger and thumb in front of the orifice of the spindle, drawing back the staple with the left hand until you have a length of about three inches

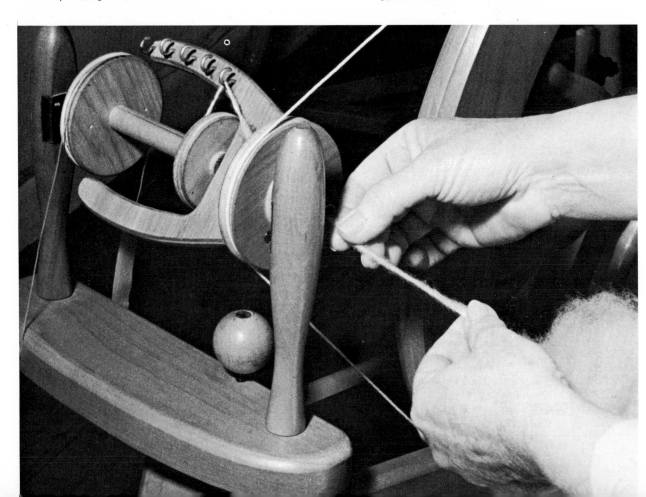

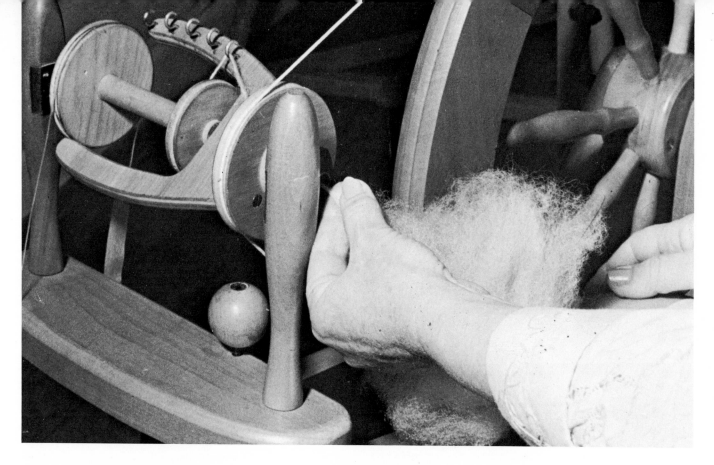

Make one full revolution of the
wheel, allowing the yarn to run
onto the bobbin

To produce a slub yarn, turn the
staple sideways and pinch out a
tuft. As confidence is gained, you
will produce the required yarn on a
steadily rotating wheel

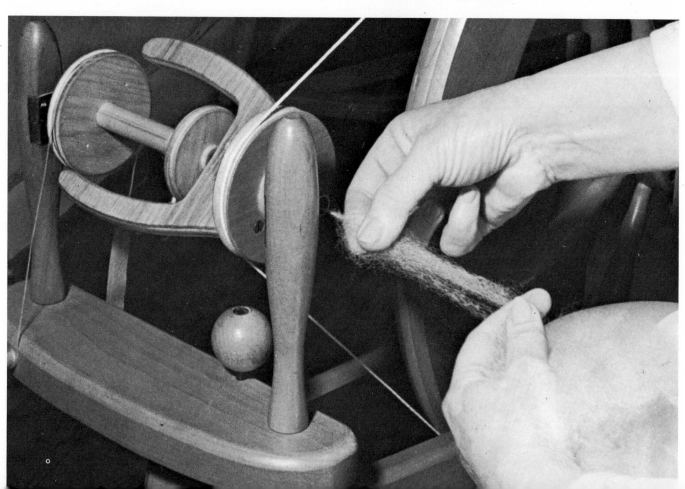

Beryl Anderson weaving on her Swedish-designed Contremarch loom. Note the spaced and grouped arrangement of the yarns in this structure of double-width fabric

Weaving a small, single corduroy pile rug. In this technique the pile weft alternately weaves and floats to some extent across the body of the warp. The floats are later cut to form the pile

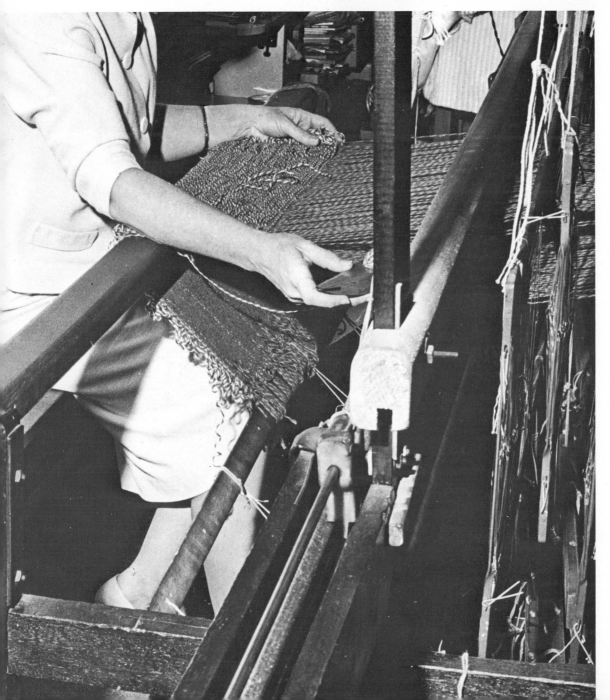

Mordanting wool before plant-dyeing

A mordant is a colour-fixative. It also helps to bring out the colour and make it fast. The mordant has a direct effect on the dye and governs the colour obtained, so that the same dye produces different colours if used with different acids or mordants. Paler shades need less mordanting than darker shades.

The beginner should be patient during the whole process of dyeing with plant material, for the secret of success lies in slow and careful work. Care in mordanting is most important; if the acid is not allowed to penetrate thoroughly into the shaft of the fibre, the colour will fade. Do not hurry the process or the results will be disappointing; your colours will not be brilliant or, if they are, they will remain only for a time and then fade.

Be sure that your yarns are completely free from grease and soap, and that the mordants are well dissolved before being mixed with the yarns. The mordanted water must be warm before the yarn is placed in. Thoroughly dissolve the mordant with boiling water in an enamel basin; pour it into the warm water in the dye bath, and stir it well. For best results the yarn should be mordanted immediately after scouring, but if this is not convenient, at least soak the wool for a couple of hours before placing it in the mordanted bath. Do not boil up quickly; very gradually increase to boiling point. Then simmer gently for from thirty minutes to an hour. The time varies according to the result desired. Do not lift the lid off the dye bath unnecessarily, for light affects mordants, though the yarn must be stirred from time to time and moved about to ensure

Colour harmony

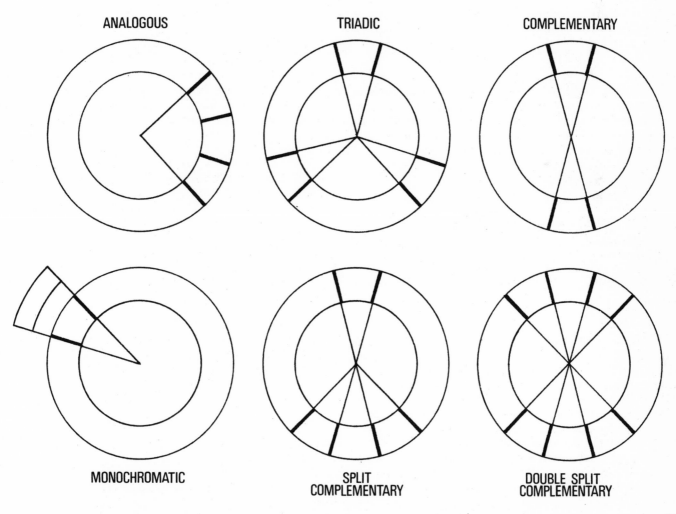

ANALOGOUS TRIADIC COMPLEMENTARY

MONOCHROMATIC SPLIT COMPLEMENTARY DOUBLE SPLIT COMPLEMENTARY

an even distribution. Allow the yarn to cool in the bath, then rinse in cool water and dry outdoors. Craftsmen declare this method of mordanting gives the best results for brightness of colour and fastness of dye.

Another method is to boil dye and mordant together in the same bath. The colour is usually bright but not always fast. A third method is to first boil the wool in the dye and then pour in the mordant to fix the colour. Boiling the wool and dye together is called "stuffing", and fixing the colour with the mordant is called "saddening".

The baths used for the processing can be enamel, aluminium, galvanized iron, or galvanized zinc. I find a four-gallon boiler a very useful size. As all my dyeing takes place on the domestic stove, the four-gallon size is convenient to handle. The yarns to be mordanted or dyed must always be well covered with water so that they can be stirred easily, and the dye or mordant can circulate thoroughly and reach each part quickly. Several wooden spoons with long handles for stirring are helpful. You will need separate baths for dyeing and mordanting and a couple of basins for dissolving mordants. You will also need several Terylene bags to hold the dye material to prevent pieces of twigs or leaves from sticking in the wool.

It is absolutely necessary, before any kind of yarn is mordanted to thoroughly wash the yarn so that no grease, dirt or soap is left in it.

Mordants

A mordant is a chemical that forms a unison between the dye and the substance to be dyed. Unless some acid is used the yarn does not absorb the dye satisfactorily and a poor-looking colour results. There are many mordants but those most frequently used are . . .

Alum (aluminum sulphate),
Chrome (bichromate of potash),
Iron sulphate (copperas, green vitriol),
Tin-crystals (stannous chloride),
Copper sulphate (verdigris, blue vitriol),
Tannic acid,
Oxalic acid,
Potassium acid tartrate (cream of tartar).

I will briefly describe the special uses and application of each.

Alum

Aluminum sulphate is used more than any other mordant though it is not as easy to deal with as bichromate of potash. It is more difficult to impregnate wool with alum. Fill a bath with enough warm water to cover the wool. Dissolve the alum with boiling water in a separate basin; pour it into the bath and stir well. Then place the damp wool in the bath. Bring slowly to boiling point and simmer gently for twenty minutes, or longer if deep colours are required.

Allow the wool to cool in the water and then rinse in warm water. While still wet put the wool into an old pillow slip and hang in a dark cupboard for at least three days. The longer it is left before preparing the dye bath the better. Two ounces of alum is sufficient for one pound of wool. Too much alum makes the wool sticky.

Potassium bichromate

This mordant is easier to deal with than alum, and the wool can be dyed immediately after mordanting. These beautiful orange-coloured crystals are poisonous and must be stored in a safe place. Dissolve the crystals in a separate bowl of boiling water, add to the bath and stir thoroughly. Place in the damp wool and bring slowly to the boil. Boil for 50 minutes. Keep the bath covered; exposure to light destroys this mordant. A quarter of an ounce is enough to mordant one pound of wool. This mordant also softens the wool.

Iron sulphate

This mordant is more difficult to apply, and unless great care is taken an uneven dye results. One quarter of an ounce is sufficient for a pound of wool. Bring to the boil gradually and boil for 30 minutes. If boiled too long the wool will harden. This mordant is sometimes added to the dye bath to darken the colour. Iron sulphate dulls bright colours, and so a special vessel should be kept for it.

Copper sulphate

This metallic compound is used as a mordant with cream of tartar, but is more commonly used as a saddening agent — the wool is dyed first and mordant used afterwards to fix the colour. By this method certain shades are obtained that would otherwise be impossible to create. Barely a quarter of an ounce to a pound of wool is required.

Tin crystals

Like copper, tin is not often used as a mordant. I do not use it as a mordant because of the hardening effect on the wool, but when added to the dye bath it is invaluable when extracting colour from a stubborn piece of bark or lichen.

It is very often used as a modifying agent with other mordants. It greatly brightens colours and helps to make them fast. When you use it as a mordant the dye bath must be quite cold before the wool is placed in. Heat gently to boiling point and boil for 30 minutes. Use a quarter of an ounce to a pound of wool.

Tannic acid

This is a very strong astringent and is used in conjunction with other mordants. It adds great brilliancy to the colours, helps to keep them fast, and is invaluable when the yarn to be dyed is a hard fibre such as linen or cotton. To treat one pound of wool, a quarter of an ounce is sufficient. Bring gently to the boil and simmer for 60 minutes. Allow the bath to become quite cold before removing the wool.

Oxalic acid

This is an excellent mordant for gaining a blue dye from berries or fruit. A beautiful lavender blue can be extracted from mulberries. A delicate shade of blue can be obtained from privet berries in a dry season. A quarter of an ounce is sufficient to mordant one pound of wool; boil gently for 60 minutes.

An interesting experiment with oxalic acid has shown that to produce the fullest shade of blue from a berry it is necessary to first mordant the wool and keep it in a cupboard for some time before using. For example, wool mordanted a month previously, when dyed with mulberries produced an exquisite shade of lavender blue. Wool used immediately after mordanting, dyed with mulberries, produced a deep shade of ginger tan.

Cream of tartar

This is not really a mordant at all. It rather adds brightness to colours. Specific recipes must be followed exactly when it is added, or the colour of the dye will be completely altered. About an ounce to the pound is generally used. Boil gently for 60 minutes.

Plant dyes

Plant dyes are excellent for their long endurance and soft, lustrous colouring. Even when very old they retain great beauty and charm, as can be seen in the old tapestries; these have faded in a uniform way, not in patches, as do fabrics dyed with manufactured dyes. It takes much longer to dye with plant dyes, but the result is excellent for really good craft work.

On the whole, plant dyes usually give soft shades, though many clear, brilliant colours can be obtained. It is often possible to produce an exact colour again and again. Yet, quite often, two people using the same recipe will not produce the same colour, though they have used the same mordant, dye, yarn and the same amount of time. Soil, climatic conditions, water, and the time of the year, will all bring a variation in colour. The craftsman is able to produce an exclusive colour, and this adds greatly to the interest of plant-dyeing.

Approximately one pound of dye material, held loosely in a Terylene bag is needed to dye one pound of wool. When experimenting with small skeins, these should be weighed and the dye stuff used in proportion. Thoroughly dissolve a large cup of salt in boiling water and pour into the dye bath with sufficient warm water to cover the wool. It is advisable to place the dye stuff in two or three (porous) Terylene bags so that it can be distributed among the wool, easily removed from the bath, and will not become entangled in the wool.

When the water of the dye bath has reached 160°F., remove the wool from the container and add about one ounce of acetic acid to the bath. The temperature is most critical, for the action of the acetic acid is unpredictable if the acid is added when the dye bath is too hot or too cold. Stir well, return the wool to the container and continue to simmer until the desired colour is obtained.

Suggestions for dyeing

A little alum is useful when extracting yellow from green leaves. The amount varies with the shade required but usually one or two ounces to every pound of dye is enough. All colours will be more permanent if Fixinol N.P. (an I.C.I. product) is used after dyeing. Rinse the wool in the Fixinol and let it stand for about fifteen minutes. Remove skeins and let them drip dry over a rod outdoors.

Interesting variations in colour and unusual effects can be obtained by . . .

1. Cramming wool into the dye bath so that the dye does not circulate evenly; the variegated yarn gives interesting effects in tapestry.
2. Putting a number of skeins, each treated with a different mordant, into the same dye bath.
3. Using wool that is not completely free from yolk or has "tippy" ends or a lot of hairy fibres. All these conditions will considerably affect the dyeing properties of the fibres.
4. Carding different colours together creates heather mixtures.
5. Over-dyeing grey fleece also makes beautiful heather mixtures.

DYEING TABLE

Plant		Mordant	Colour
African marigold:		alum	greenish yellow
flowers		alum & cream of tartar	fawn yellow
		iron	greenish grey
		chrome	old gold brown
		tin	bright yellow
Ageratum: flowers		alum	primrose
		chrome	deep fawn
		tin	bright yellow
		iron	bright green
Banana: flowers		oxalic acid	gold
Beetroot: beet		alum	apricot
		cream of tartar	pale yellow
Begonia: red flowers		chrome	deep peach
		cream of tartar	mauve
Blackberry:	fruit	oxalic acid	blue
	fruit	oxalic acid & tin	ginger tan
	leaves	alum & tin	deep grey
Broad beans		tin	canary yellow
		chrome	fawn
		iron	grey green
Broom: flowers & stems		alum	yellow
		chrome	gold
Calendula: flowers		alum	canary yellow
Canna: red flowers		tin	orange tan
Coral tree: flowers		chrome	green
		tannic acid	London tan
		iron	deep tan

Plant	Mordant	Colour
Cow parsley: leaves & stems	alum	green
Cox comb: leaves & stems	alum	deep apricot yellow
	iron	light grey
Dahlia: orange flowers	alum	orange
Dock: leaves & stems	alum	bright canary yellow
	chrome	bronze green
French marigold: flowers	alum	brown green
Hawthorn: orange berries	chrome	pearl grey
Japonica: flowers	oxalic acid	blue
Lasiandra: flowers	iron	medium grey
	alum & cream of tartar	grey
Mulberry: berries	iron	purplish plum
	tannic acid	pink cinnamon
	chrome	geranium leaf green
	cream of tartar	rust
	oxalic acid	lavender blue & tan
Mulberry: leaves	various mordants	light yellow to orange tan
Nettles: leaves & stems	alum	greenish yellow
Onions (brown): skins	alum	rust
	tin	orange
	iron & alum	olive green
Passionfruit: skins	alum	purple grey
Pittosporum: berries (best when bursting and resinous)	chrome	greenish yellow
	alum	gold
	alum & chrome	nigger brown
Pomegranate: fruit	iron	mauve grey
	tannic acid	fawn
Privet: berries	iron	light grey
	copper sulphate	fawn
	alum	light green
	oxalic acid	blue
	chrome	green
Prunus: leaves & stems	iron	moss green
Rhubarb: leaves	alum	deep yellow
Seaweed: any variety	chrome	sage green
	cream of tartar & tin	dark gold
	oxalic acid	light gold
	tannic acid	fawn
Spinach: leaves	alum	greenish yellow
Tomatoes (tree): red	cream of tartar & tin	mauve blue
Wattle: sprays (just before flowering)	chrome	green
	alum	gold
	oxalic acid	bright yellow
Usnea (old man's beard)	alum	light yellow
	chrome	green
	oxalic acid	brownish green
	unmordanted	fawn, orange, brown

Plant (barks)	Mordant	Colour
Camphor laurel	chrome	rich pinky fawn
Iron bark	tannic acid	orange tan
Wattle	alum & cream of tartar	mid rust
Box	alum	pinky fawn
Iron bark	chrome & tin	bronze

Plant (lichens)	Mordant	Colour
Orange lichen	alum	brilliant yellow
	oxalic acid	brilliant yellow
	tannic acid	tan
	chrome	rich golden tan
	unmordanted	gold
Parmelia arnoldii	tannic acid	rich reddish tan
	alum	pinky fawn

(Your local chemist will advise you on how to purchase mordants.)

Insect dye (cochineal)

I have included three recipes for dyeing with Coccus cacti or cochineal — an animal-based dye that gives unusual shades of red and scarlet. Although cochineal crystals are obtainable my experiments were made with liquid cochineal food colouring.

Salmon pink:
1 pound of wool (mordanted with alum)
¼ oz. stannous chloride
1 oz. oxalic acid
2 oz. cochineal
Dissolve chemicals and pour cochineal in bath together.
Bring slowly to the boil. Boil for 2 hours.

Tomato red:
1 pound of handspun mordanted with alum
4 oz. alum
2 oz. cream of tartar
½ oz. stannous chloride
8 oz. cochineal
Dissolve mordants and boil all together for 2 hours.

Carmine:
1 pound handspun mordanted with alum
4 oz. alum
4 oz. cream of tartar
4 oz. cochineal
Dissolve mordants and boil all together for 2 hours.

These dyes are very quick to use. Many shades ranging from salmon pink, through to red and violet can be obtained with cochineal.

knitting with handspun

Many knitters want to spin their own yarn, so here is some information about patterns, stitch gauges, blocking and the essentials of well-fitting garments. There is a growing interest in knitwear, and luxurious and elegant knitted garments as well as practical outfits are being worn. New ways have opened for knitting handspun natural fibres, such as wool, cotton, flax, dog combings, goat and rabbit hair, and silk. The problem is how to use these novel yarns to create a particular design.

Measurements and shaping

Too many knitters rely on stereotyped directions, with the result that the work is often too big or too small and generally unsatisfactory. In the first place, you may wish to use different yarns and needles, so the work may be tighter or looser than expected; and few of us are a perfect size 12 or 14. A garment that appears in an attractively illustrated knitting book may be exactly what you desire, with the exception of the neckline or waist-band. It is a simple matter to change these details if you strictly adhere to size measurements and accuracy with the stitch gauge.

The stitch gauge

This is the name given to the number of stitches to the inch and rows to the inch, measured on a piece of stockinette stitch made with a known yarn on known needles. The gauge depends upon the yarn knitted, the size of the needles and the tension given by the knitter. Difficulty is encountered in the fit of knitted wear partly because of an inaccurate stitch gauge and partly because of not knowing how to take the necessary measurements for the garment.

Make a chart for yourself by taking the following measurements: length (measured from the socket bone at the back of the neck), front bust or chest, across the back underarm, combined front and back measurement, waist, and waist to underarm. Also take measurements of the shoulder to shoulder, wrist, upper arm, forearm, sleeve length under arm, and armhole.

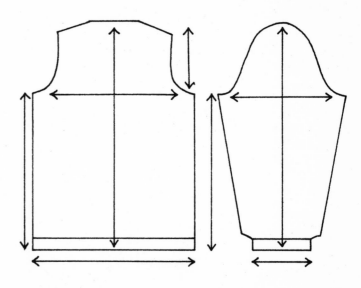

Measurement chart

The body measurements given in many knitting books are sometimes confusing. It is not simply body measurements you need for knit design, but the necessary measurements for the finished garment for a particular person. No blocking will ever stop a skirt from cupping if the necessary width has not been added for the hips.

One of the best methods I know to ensure accurate fitting of a knitted garment by the home knitter, if you do not trust yourself to draft your own patterns, is to invest in a basic pattern, cut and fitted for you by a professional dressmaker. You may knit any style of garment with the assurance that it is going to fit perfectly without cutting or stretching. When drafting a pattern, the final measurements are to be used. Therefore the stitch gauge will be the same as when the garment is worn. Become accustomed to the small amount of stretch a material has when it is flattened.

At the beginning I advise steaming the piece of fabric (this does not mean pinning it down, for it might be pinned to many sizes). Simply steam over the piece, on the wrong side, using a steam iron, keeping the weight of the iron in the hand. Now it will be the size required for the finished fabric.

To make a "stitch gauge" knit a sample piece of fabric. With the yarn and needles that are to be used for the garment, cast on 20 stitches and knit a piece of stockinette stitch (knit one row, purl one row, for 20 rows). The thicker the yarn, the fewer stitches necessary. The heavier the yarn, the greater the possible error. Steam the piece of stockinette material, then count the number of stitches and the number of rows to the inch. Do not measure the loops on the needle, but measure the extent of the work itself.

Half a stitch makes a big difference when measuring stitches to the inch. For instance, a piece of knitting 12" long, 6 stitches to the inch, requires 72 stitches. But 12 inches at 6½ to the inch, needs 78 stitches — a difference of 6 stitches, which is important in the fit of a garment.

Use stockinette stitch for the gauge, whatever the texture stitch to be used in the garment.

Blocking

A sweater knitted with correct measurements should not have to be blocked. It should just be steamed flat. But for knitters who wish to block the finished garment, you will need a pad for a base on which the garment may be pinned.

Turn the garment inside out and with pins mark the centre-back of the sweater. On the blocking pad, place the pins at A and B, where the centre-back is to be pinned to the pad. Pin the waist through the basque C to D using half the waist measurement — one quarter on each side of AB. In a cardigan the centre-back and sides are pinned before the fronts are pinned. At D measure DF, which is the underarm to waist measurement. Measure EF, which is half the bust measurement — one quarter on each side of AB.

Spread the armholes correctly and pin to the pad. Test the shoulders for correct width, adjust the neck-line and pin in position. Measure the sleeve underarm length, check the width, pin to pad, then steam. Never steam ribbing, since the garment should not be stretched.

Knitting a rugged ski cardigan

The yarn in the cardigan (see colour photo), is spun from a Crossbred black fleece, plied and over-dyed with a bright orange aniline dye. The colours in the fleece ranged from pale grey to deep charcoal. Consequently, when over-dyed with orange, the colours ranged from a deep rust through to orange. One and a half ounces of dye to three pounds of wool produced the desired strength.

The directions for knitting have been worked out very carefully; and to ensure a perfect fitting it is essential, before commencing to knit, to test your tension.

Directions are given here for the cardigan in four bust sizes, standard measurements.

Bust measurement:	32ins.	34ins.	36ins.	38ins.
Actual measurement of garment:	34ins.	36ins.	38ins.	40ins.
Sleeve seam:	17½ins.	18ins.	18ins.	18ins.
Material required:	15 skeins	16 skeins	16 skeins	18 skeins

The skeins weigh approximately 3 ounces each. You will need one pair each of size 5 and size 8 needles and 7 buttons. The tension is 4 stitches and 5 rows to 1 inch. Using size 5 needles, measure tension over stockinette stitch.

Abbreviations

k.= knit, p.= purl, st.= stitch, sts.= stitches, ins.= inches, rep.= repeat, beg.= beginning, sl.= slip, tog.= together, st.st.= stocking stitch, psso.= pass slipped stitch over, inc.= increase, dec.= decrease.

Instructions are given for the smallest size, with the larger sizes in brackets.

Back

Using size 8 needles cast on 68 (72, 76, 80) sts.
Work in (k.1, p.1) rib for 8 rows.
Change to size 5 needles and st.st. (k.1 row, p.1 row) until back measures 13½ (14, 14, 14) ins. or the required length, from the beginning. End with a p. row. If making the jacket longer, extra wool will be required.

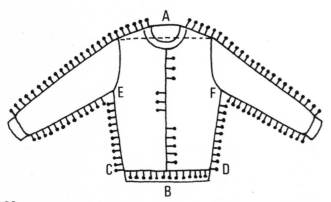

Blocking a knitted cardigan

Shape raglan armholes

*Next row k.3, sl.1, k.1, psso., k. to last 5 sts., k.2 tog., k.3.
Next row p.
Repeat the last 2 rows * until 20 (22, 22, 24) sts. remain, ending with a p. row. Leave these sts. on a spare needle.

Left front

Using size 8 needles cast on 34 (36, 38, 40) sts.
Work in (k.1, p.1) rib for 8 rows. Change to size 5 needles and st.st. Work until front measures 13½ (14, 14, 14) ins. or the required length, from the beginning. End with a p. row.

Shape raglan armhole

Next row k.3, sl.1, k.1, psso., k. to end.
Next row p.
Rep. the last 2 rows until 17 (18, 18, 19) sts. remain.

Shape neck

Next row cast off 5 (6, 6, 7) sts. p. to end.
Dec. 1 st. at neck edge on the next and every following alternate row, 4 times. At the same time continue to dec. 1 st. at armhole edge as before, until 1 st. remains. Work armhole decreases at outer armhole edge when they can no longer be worked inside a border of 3 sts. Fasten off.

Right front

Follow instructions for left front, reversing shapings and armhole. Dec. row will be k. to the last 5 sts. k.2 tog., k.3.

Sleeves

Using size 8 needles, cast on 44 (46, 48, 50) sts. Work in (k.1, p.1) rib for 16 rows. Change to size 5 needles and st.st. Inc. 1 st. at each end of the 11th and every following 12th (12th, 10th, 10th) row until there are 54, (56, 60, 62) sts. on the needle. Continue without further shaping until sleeve measures 17½ (18, 18, 18) ins. from the beg. or required length, ending with a p. row.

Shape raglan top

Follow instructions for back from * to * until 6 sts. remain, working decreases at outer armhole edge when they can no longer be worked inside a border of 3 sts. End with a p. row. Leave these 6 sts. on a safety pin.

Buttonhole band

Using size 8 needles, cast on 9 sts.
1st row * k.1, p.1 rep. from * to last st., then k.1.
2nd row * p.1, k.1 rep. from * to last st., then p.1.
Repeat these 2 rows for 1 (½, ¾, 1) inch.
1st buttonhole row rib 3, cast off 3, rib to end.
2nd buttonhole row rib, casting on over cast off sts. in previous row.
Work more buttonholes at intervals of 3 (3¼, 3¼, 3¼) ins. measured from base of previous buttonhole. Work a further 2½ (2¾, 2¾, 2¾) ins. in rib. Leave these sts. on a safety pin.

Button band

Work to match buttonhole band, omitting buttonholes.

Collar

Using a flat stitch, join raglan seams. Using size 8 needles rib across the 9 sts. on buttonhole band, pick up and k. 20 (21, 22, 23) sts. up right side of neck. k.6 sts. from top of one sleeve. k.20 (22, 22, 24) sts. from back neck, inc. into last st. k.6 sts. from top of second sleeve. Pick up and k.20 (21, 22, 23) sts. down left side of neck, rib across the 9 sts. on button band 91 (95, 97, 101) sts.
Next row * p.1, k.1 rep. from * to last st. p.1.
Continue in rib for 1½ ins., making the 7th buttonhole 3 (3¼, 3¼, 3¼) ins. from the base of previous buttonhole.
Change to size 5 needles and work a further 4 ins. in rib.
Cast off in rib. Make garment up according to previous directions.

ACKNOWLEDGEMENTS

I would like to thank the Australian Wool Board Special Projects Section for their co-operation in supplying photographs and statistical information; and also Gay Ashford for lending ski-wear from her collection of home-spun knitwear.

Suppliers

Fleece, mohair and cotton

Grazcos Co-operative Limited, Euston Road, Alexandria, N.S.W. supply all breeds of fleece; contact Mr J. M. Jenkins for assistance and advice. Mr A. Cowen, 33 Cuzco Street, South Coogee, N.S.W. breeds and supplies white and coloured mohair. The Namoi Cotton Co-operative Limited, P.O. Box 58, Wee Waa, N.S.W. supplies raw cotton.

Spinning wheels and handweaving appliances

Spinners and Weavers Supplies, Box 186 Double Bay, N.S.W. has a wide range of handweaving appliances and spinning wheels. Mr J. H. Wilson, 44 Minter Street, Canterbury, N.S.W. supplies spinning and handweaving appliances and Upright spinning wheels. Ashford Handicrafts Limited, P.O. Box 412, Rakaia, Canterbury, New Zealand supplies spinning wheels. David Jones Limited, Wool Department, Elizabeth Street, Sydney, N.S.W. supplies Ashford spinning wheels.

Striking double-breasted coat hand-woven from machine and handspun Cheviot wool

Mixing wool with other fibres: a room divider woven in brilliantly dyed, opaque stripes of tightly spun Cheviot wool and open mesh. The Spanish lace design is executed with Manilla rope

Sports coat handwoven from novelty-spun Crossbred natural black fleece, with deliberately spun thick and thin yarn

Floor rug of Corriedale and Border
Leicester wools. Handwoven from
unpsun fleece of natural colour

Beryl Anderson removing wool from carding machine. It is operated by a small handle on the side — or it can easily be motorized by a handyman

Spinning the yarn: Filia Dragani, of Salonika, now residing in Australia, demonstrates the art of spinning wool with a spindle

Curtain material of Border Leicester, a strong wool with a deep crimp. When spun sideways from the staple, the crimps develop an unusual twist that becomes a very handsome novelty-spun yarn in a single ply. The curtains are dyed with mulberry leaves

Room divider of novelty-spun Border Leicester and Cheviot wools, with sections of unwoven warp, creating a light airy effect

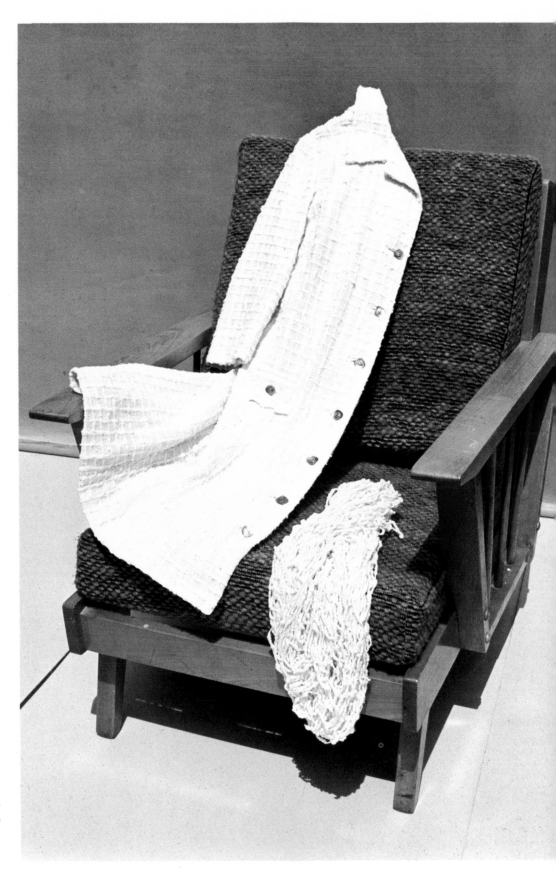

Handwoven dress spun from raw cotton. The cotton fibres have minute kinks and twists and, by means of these irregularities, they cling together when spun

Handwoven dress of handspun raw silk from India, in the "frisson" stage of silk preparation — regarded as the best form of silk for the handspinner

Handspun, handwoven flax: the fibres are deliberately spun for a special effect. Novelty spun yarns are used here in conjunction with precise, evenly spun yarns

This bedspread is woven from unspun Border Leicester fleece in shades of natural black and gold. The dyes are extracted from pittosporum berries

Ski-wear: Janelle's jumper is handspun and knitted from natural black fleece. Larry's rugged cardigan is spun from a crossbred black fleece, over-dyed with a bright orange aniline dye

Novelty-spun yarns in these travelling rugs are dyed with various plant materials — lichens, mulberries, leaves and bark. Fleeces used are Cheviot, Dorset Horn, Polwarth and Border Leicester

Sweater woven with handspun wool from a Corriedale fleece, using both natural and coloured wool

This coat is characteristic of the natural approach of the ancient Peruvians to costume design. Shaped on the loom, the process in itself is simple, but careful attention must be paid to measurements and allowance made for take-up and shrinkage

Divan cover: threading and treadling orders are the same as those
given for the double-width curtain.
The weft is Border Leicester. Dyed
in the fleece and colour-blended,
the wool is carded and laid in the
shed by "finger-weaving"

Sun-room curtains, with a comparatively low-cost design. Sufficiently translucent to allow the maximum of light at all times and heavy enough to protect from the sun's rays when needed, these curtains would be excellent for entirely curtaining a sun-room

Double-width curtain fabric: handspun from Border Leicester, a strong wool with a deep crimp. When spun sideways from the staple, the crimps develop an unusual twist, that becomes a very handsome novelty-spun yarn in a single ply

Cushion of a tubular fabric: tubular designs are unusual and exciting. This cushion shows an example of deliberately-spun textures and beautiful colour blending

Travelling rugs offer endless possibilities for design. Sensitively woven in natural materials with an inherent beauty, this rug is both functional and attractive and provides the handweaver with one of the most satisfying pieces of craft work that can be created from the loom

Woven quexquemetl: these delightfully zany quexquemetls may be woven in an evening and make very acceptable gifts. The unspun wool is vividly dyed in colour-harmonizing shades